ANTO

Bols

and the Towns around the Lake

New practical guide

120 color photos
Tradition and folklore
Day outings
Useful information
City map

BONECHI EDIZIONI "IL TURISMO"

"...reflected in the pearl hued lake,
smooth as glass it mirrors, crystal clear, the sky,
which seems to pass through and continue
beneath the golden ring with two isles
two aerial ships suspended in infinity".

(Corrado Ricci, 1928).

*T*he origins of Bolsena go back to time imme-
morial, when a lake, surrounded by a crown of
hills covered with luxuriant wild vegetation, was
formed as a result of volcanic activity. When geologi-
cal activity subsided, man began to settle on the shores
and slopes, and traces of some of these settlements
have come down to us.

▲ Bolsena seen from the lake

◄ Remains of volcanic cones

► Remains of the Etruscan-Roman wall of Bolsena

The first indications of human presence on the shores of the lake date to the middle Paleolithic. We know more about the Bronze and Iron Age, with clusters of dwellings along the shores and numer-

▲ The characteristic "pietre lanciate"
or "thrown stones",
a curious phenomenon of volcanic origin

ous pottery finds that can be attributed to the Villanovan culture (9th-early 8th cent. B.C.), with settlements of considerable scientific and archaeological interest in the localities of Grancar, Civita d'Arlena and Monte Bisenzio.

The Etruscans left only modest signs of their presence in Bolsena,

▲ Old Roman road to Bolsena

▼ Grotto of Santa Cristina

with a small fortified settlement and a few tombs dating to the 7th-6th century B.C.

When the Romans definitively destroyed the Etruscan Velzna (now Orvieto) in 264 B.C., the survivors moved to the north-eastern shores of the lake of Bolsena, and a second Velzna sprang up in a location not as easily defended as the preceding. Thanks to its position on the tract of the Via Cassia it developed and became a municipium with the name of Volsinii.

Important early Christian evidence, such as the Catacombs of Santa Cristina and those of Grotte (used in the 4th and 5th century) document the presence of a rather large and active Christian community in the town, that sprang

▲ The medieval castle of Bolsena

up around the cult of Saint Cristina, although it remained strongly attached to its pagan traditions.

Bolsena was razed to the ground by the Lombards in the second half of the 6th century. The survivors of these terrible raids abandoned the Roman city and built a new town up on the cliff where the medieval quarter still stands today.

At the end of Lombard domination, Bolsena became part of the possessions of the Church under the diocese of Orvieto of which it became to all extents a property.

In 1263, with Pope Urban IV in Orvieto, the Eucharistic Miracle took place in Bolsena, and its fame quickly spread throughout the Christian world and led the pope to institute the church feast day of Corpus Christi.

During the Renaissance the sto-

▼ The Monaldeschi palace *and*
a fascinating view of Bolsena towards the lake

ry of our city moves parallel to that of the papacy. It was in this period that illustrious personages such as Cardinal Giovanni de' Medici, future Leo X, Cardinal Tiberio Crispo, Pius II Piccolomini and Paul III Farnese were guests in the city.

Our itinerary begins, descending along the Via Orvietana, at Poggio Moscini, with the visit to the remains of the Roman city of *Volsinii* where the archaeological digs have brought to light numerous significant monumental remains of the urbanized area. They are located in the lower part of the urban perimeter, with the *amphitheater of Mercatello* on the north. The *Forum* has a paving of square slabs, many of which were removed in various periods to be used in other structures such as the fortress and its principal tower (13th-14th cent.), the reorganization of the Borgo and the facade of the Church of Santa Cristina (15th cent.) and for Cardinal Crispo's constructions. On some of the slabs, engravings of an early Christian period seem to indicate that the area was utilized at the time for funerary purposes. There were once many more column shafts in pink granite than those now to be seen in an unpaved area. Most of these columns belonged to the facade of the *Civic Basilica*, of Flavian period, one of the most important public buildings of *Volsinii*. Even though these no longer exist, there is no doubt

▼ Archaeological area of Poggio Moscini

▲ Archaeological area of Poggio Moscini

as to their identification. The Basilica, divided into three aisles, consisted of a vast four-sided area next to the Forum. There was a podium at the northwest end, probably seat of the magistrature. Civic basilicas were reserved for judicial and administrative activities, as well as commercial, monetary and banking negotiations. In the early 4th century this civic basilica was transformed into a Christian basilica church, and an apse was built on an axis with the nave.

Of particular interest on the stretch of *road* flanking the basilica are two large raised stones, like those frequently to be seen in the streets of Pompeii where they served as pedestrian crossings. Passing through what must have been a small portico, one can observe the *shops*, datable to the early 1st cent. B.C., one of which, dug into the rock, has niches in the tufa wall and a rudimentary paving.

◄ Remains of a capital in Corinthian style

▶ Detail of a frescoed wall in the House of the Paintings

Returning to the road that flanks the Forum, an entrance leads into the *Vaulted Passageway,* once completely covered and forming a closed corridor between the Forum and the terraces below. The polygonal stone paving is still intact.

Moving a few meters up on the right after leaving the vaulted passageway takes us to the *Tre botteghe* or Three Shops. This was a busy zone, to judge from the grooves in the cobblestones, and was where the shops serving the people on their way to the Forum were located.

The *House of the Paintings (Casa delle Pitture)* is reached by descending a small modern staircase. This is a typical *domus*, with an atrium, of which only

▼ Detail of a frescoed wall in the House of the Paintings

▲ Domus with Atrium, marble pavement
(opus sectile)

the central basin or *impluvium* remains, with the *tablinum* or living room, still with part of its black and white mosaic carpet, opposite. To the left of the tablinum is a large hall with paving of different periods that probably served as a *triclinium* or dining room. On the northeast was a garden that was replaced around the middle of the 2nd century by a small peristyle of which nothing remains today.

The rooms of imperial period are in an excellent state of preservation and the painted plaster walls are of particular interest. The white ground is divided into geometric frames containing colored images of birds, a bowl of fruit, stylized plant motifs.

From one of these rooms, following the *dromos* (a corridor sloping downwards) where a checkerboard wall changes to bare rock, one arrives at a subterranean room. This very old construction (late 3rd century B.C.) was earlier than the *domus* and can therefore not be interpreted as a simple cistern but, probably, as a place reserved for the worship of Dionysus. The numerous terracotta fragments found here that were reconstructed and formed a Dionysian throne with panthers (*Panther Throne*), now in the Museo Territoriale of Bolsena, support this hypothesis.

◄ Domus with Atrium, washing basin

In a zone that seems not to have been built up, attention is drawn to the well-preserved *washing basin*. Water descending from a *nymphaeum* (monumental fountain), part of the *domus* on the terrace above, was collected in a fountain that had a niche in the wall at the back, and a bench covered in flat tiles where the laundry was beaten. On the ground, a marble catch basin served as drain.

Other important vestiges belong to the *Domus with Atrium*, with various interesting rooms. One in particular has a fine pavement in marble mosaic (*opus sectile*).

The *Domus* includes a nymphaeum consi- sting of a long open courtyard, closed on two sides by tall walls in which niches have been dug. The water gushed forth in jets and went into a circular tub.

The construction of the *nymphaeum* compromised pre-existing structures, such as the *Small temple* (second half of the 2nd cent. B.C.) to which a square foundation in large stones bears witness. A round plastered altar was set before what must have been the front of the sacred building. A terracotta statue of Venus and oil lamps were found on the altar.

► Domus with Atrium, detail of the *nymphaeum*

13

Leaving the digs of Poggio Moscini and continuing along the Via Orvietana towards the historical center we encounter, almost immediately, the *Fortress* or *Rocca Monaldeschi della Cervara,* rising majestically at the top of an outcrop that dominates the medieval quarter. It was built in various stages, from the 11th to the 14th century, when the Monaldeschi della Cervara turned it into a bulwark of their rule over Bolsena.

The irregular ground plan is trapezoidal and four slender towers rise up at the corners, no two alike. They reveal the original Gothic structure of the building and are framed by regular projections supported by dentiled brackets and depressed arches.

The rooms of the Rocca Mo-

▲ The Rocca Monaldeschi della Cervara

◄ Porta Fiorentina and further up, left, the Palazzo del Drago

▼ Typical lane in the medieval hamlet

naldeschi today house the **Museo Territoriale del Lago di Bolsena**, entrance to which is through a courtyard containing funerary stele and altars. The museum is divided into six sections, one of which is purely didactic and reconstructs the history of the lake and the civilizations that rose and developed around it.

The didactic section, using models, drawings and panels, illustrates the various phases of the formation of the territory that began hundreds of thousands of years ago with the appearance of the great volcanoes. The section devoted to protohisto-

▼ Museo del Lago: the *Panther Throne and* detail of a tub-shaped sarcophagus dating to the 2nd-3rd cent. A.D.

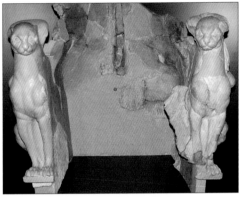

▲ The glacis of the Fortress (Rocca) provide a sweeping view of the lake

ry also documents the Villanovan settlements with interesting archaeological finds, as well as panels.

The showcases of the Etruscan section contain finds from the tombs in the area around the lake.

Of interest in the part of the museum devoted to the Roman culture is the *Panther Throne,* used in the cult of Dionysus and found in the archaeological digs of Poggio Moscini, as well as pottery vessels, oil lamps and paintings.

The other sections illustrate the history of the medieval hamlet of Bolsena, with particular attention to the economic activity and the naturalistic aspects of the lake: the flora, fauna, morphological features. There are also panels that explain in detail the fishing activities of the lake, illustrating equipment and terminology.

At the end of the visit to the museum a climb to the glacis

◀ The facade of the former Church of San Francesco

forms in honor of the Nativity of the Virgin.

Later, after the approval of the Franciscan Order, the church was rededicated to Saint Francis and the original Romanesque forms were replaced by an elegant Gothic, still to be seen in the fine portal.

of the Fort provides the visitor with a sweeping view of the lake.

After leaving the Rocca Monaldeschi, the ruins of the city walls are the last vestiges of the original nucleus of ancient *Volsinii*. Moving down along the winding Via Orvietana we arrive in Piazza Matteotti, with the sober and elegant *Church of San Francesco*. It was built at the beginning of the 13th century in Romanesque

The strikingly simple interior consists of a nave only ending in a square apse and with a trussed roof. Completely restructured and deconsecrated, it has been transformed into a large

► Ippolito Scalza's sixteenth-century arch

theater structure and is now used for cultural activities.

Passing under the sixteenth century *arch* by Ippolito Scalza, one reaches Piazza San Rocco, crossing the *Borgo* or town center (Corso Cavour). The Renaissance *fountain* here has small pilasters decorated in relief, the only surviving decorative elements of late fifteenth-century fountain, probably by the school of Benedetto Buglioni, in the period in which he was working on the facade of the Church of Santa Cristina. The original fountain, polygonal in shape, was at the center of the square.

Returning to Piazza Matteotti we move along Corso della Repubblica towards Piazza Santa Cristina, with the fine *Palazzo of Cardinal Teodorico* in simple Gothic lines built at the end of the 12th century, and the splendid *Basilica of Santa Cristina*.

This architectural complex consists of four distinct parts: the small underground basi-

▼ Piazza San Rocco
and the fountain of San Rocco

▲ Palazzo of Cardinal Teodorico

▶ The Basilica of Santa Cristina

lica known as *Grotto of Santa Cristina* and the *catacombs*, the three-aisled *Romanesque building*, the *Chapel of the Miracle* and the *Chapel of San Leonardo*.

The oldest part of the complex consists of the *catacombs* and the *Grotto of Santa Cristina*, thought to be the original place where the saint was honored (although, as it is today, the structure dates to the 10th century). It seems in fact that the body of the young martyr, victim of the persecutions of Diocletian (late 3rd cent.), was buried by her Christian companions in a tomb in the catacombs. Subsequently an altar was erected on the site of her grave. In the early 16th century, a fine terracotta statue was set on the place where the body of the Saint is buried. Attributed to Benedetto Buglioni, it shows the young martyr sleeping the sleep of death. Popular tradition has it that Cristina, daughter of the prefect Urbano, was converted to the Christian faith against her father's will. He submitted her to cruel tortures from which the young girl always came out unharmed glorifying God. Af-

The Mysteries of Santa Cristina

The most spectacular and import event in Bolsena from the point of view of historical and cultural traditions is the representation of the *Mysteries*.

As sacred representations they probably originated in the Middle Ages, modeled on the "*Passion*" of Saint Cristina, dating to the 5th century.

The evening of July 23rd, the simulacrum of the Saint is transferred from the basilica church that bears her name to the Church of Santissimo Salvatore, in the Castello district. As the procession that accompanies the statue moves on, the tortures the child martyr was subject to, are represented as "living pictures" (with a few exceptions) on five stages set up along the route.

On the morning of the 24th, the procession retraces its steps and five other martyrs are represented on the stages used the evening before.

The scenes usually shown are:

▲ Fresco
in the catacombs of Santa Cristina

the wheel, the furnace, the boulder, the lake, the devils, the whips, and the serpents, the cutting of the tongue, the arrows, and the burial.

In the course of the centuries these scenes have changed somewhat, with the exception of those with devils and serpents that appear in the oldest descriptions of these events.

Undoubtedly the scene of the martyrdom with serpents is the most spectacular since real snakes are used.

Hundreds of local people participate in this event, in particular the young, proudly committed to keeping up a tradition that has continued uninterruptedly throughout the course of centuries.

ter Urbano's death, his successors Dione and Giulano continued to torment Cristina hoping to get her to abjure, but she continued to come through unharmed, until finally an arrow passed through her heart on the 24th of July of an unspecified year in the reign of Diocletian.

The corridors of the catacombs branch out from the underground basilica. Part of this haunting early Christian necropolis was destroyed when the small basilica church was built. Like all cemeteries in antiquity, it stood right outside the urban area, near a road that seems to have been the old Via Cassia. The many inscriptions in the catacombs, ranging from simple graffiti on plaster to verse and prose and paintings, are evidence that both the humble classes and the higher social classes had embraced Christianity. Our necropolis dates from the last years of the 3rd to the first decade of the 5th century.

The *Altar* known as *of the Miracle* is at the center of the Grotto of Santa Cristina. It incorporates the stone on which, according to a devoted tradition, the Saint left the imprint of her feet. The pyramidal *Ciborium*, dating to between the 8th and 9th century, is supported by four columns in pink marble, with capitals in Corinthian style. The stone balustrade that surrounds the altar dates to the middle of the 16th century.

The *Altar of the Miracle* or *of the Four Columns* is connected to the Eucharistic Miracle that took place in 1263 when, according to tradition, a Bohemian priest tormented by doubts as to the real presence of Christ in the Eucharist, went in pilgrima-

▼ View of the Grotto of Santa Cristina

▲ The Altar of the Miracle

▼ The Reliquary containing one of the "Holy Stones" of the Eucharistic Miracle

▲ Basalt stone with the impression of the feet of Saint Cristina

ge to Rome. Pausing in Bolsena, he said mass on the tomb of Saint Cristina. It seems that at the moment of consecration, drops of blood issued forth from the host the unbelieving priest was holding, staining the altar cloth or corporal and some of the stones in the floor. These

◀ Interior of the Basilica of Santa Cristina

▼ Eighteenth-century altarpiece by Sebastiano Conca

stones are now in the Baroque Chapel known as *of the Miracle* while the corporal is in the Cathedral of Orvieto.

In the adjacent *Chapel of San Michele* is a ceramic altarpiece depicting the *Crucifixion* (1496) attributed to Benedetto Buglioni.

The central part of the architectural complex of the basilica dates to the year 1078 and was traditionally built by Matilde of Canossa and Pope Gregory VII on an earlier religious building.

The Latin-cross construction has a nave and two aisles with a truss roof. The original Romanesque style is evident in the interior with its bare simplicity and rude convex columns, in part from piers of Roman buildings. Behind the high altar is a fine *polyptych* by Sano di Pietro (1406-1481). The *Chapel* known as *of Santa Lucia* contains a terracotta bust attributed to Benedetto Buglioni and fine frescoes (late 15th century), by Domenico di Giovanni De Ferrariis da Mondovì. After being moved here and there and carefully restored, the ceramic *Ciborium*, a fine piece by the Florentine sculptor Benedetto Buglioni, has found its final and appropriate place in the *Chapel of the SS. Sacramento*.

Of particular artistic interest are the three eighteenth-century *altarpieces*, by Francesco Trevisani, Sebastiano Conca and Andrea Casali.

The facade of the Romanesque church da-

tes to the end of the 15th century and was built for Cardinal Giovanni de' Medici, the future Leo X. The decorated pilaster strips that divide the facade into three parts are crossed by a trapezoidal cornice.

The central portal of the church and that of the *Chapel of San Leonardo*, to the right of the church itself, are surmounted by lunettes with elegant terracottas, again by the Florentine Benedetto Buglioni.

► Lunette of the central portal of the Basilica with the *Madonna and Child and Saints Cristina and George*, by Benedetto Buglioni

▼ Decorative pilaster strip on the facade of the basilica

TRADITION AND FOLKLORE IN BOLSENA

The "infiorate of Corpus Domini"

(Flower carpets of the feast of Corpus Christi)

Every year for the feast of Corpus Christi the entire historical center of Bolsena is carpeted in a floral tapestry around two kilometers long spread out along the route of the procession, including the narrow lanes of the medieval quarter. This floral decoration is the fruit of the initiative of a group of citizens who gather the flowers and then design and execute the decorations. The flowers are gathered a few days before the festivities, usually early in the morning when their freshness and fragrance has not yet been withered by the sun. They are then kept in cool dark places until they are needed.

The most commonly used flowers are broom, acacia (flowers and leaves), roses, forget-me-nots, briar roses, clover, thistle flowers, vetch and hop, ferns. The designs, generally the simple repetition of geometric figures, rarely figural, are sketched out on paper or, the same day, on the paving. The designs are outlined on the ground either with coffee grounds, sawdust

The bell tower (13th cent.) rises, slender and elegant, with three tiers of two-light openings.

The *Cappella Nuova del Miracolo*, in remembrance of the Eucharistic Miracle, was built at the end of the 17th century in the area of the large courtyard on which the facade of the Grotto of Santa Cristina originally faced.

The interior of the chapel, round in plan, is in an imposing Baroque style. The marble stones stained with the blood from the host are on the high altar. The fine *painting* of the *Miracle of Bolsena* is by Francesco Trevisani (18th century). The neoclassic facade of the chapel dates to 1863.

painted black or with chestnut inflorescences steeped in water. The various parts of the design are then filled in with flowers or flower petals, and sprinkled every so often with water so they will not be blown away by the wind.

The fruit of this dedicated work, that sometimes begins late in the morning and continues till late afternoon, is short-lived. When the procession arrives, in particular when the Blessed Sacrament passes, the floral carpet is trodden on and all that remains on the ground are indistinct spots of color and a unique and ineffable fragrance.

▼ Interior
of the Cappella Nuova del Miracolo

The shores of the lake can be reached by returning to Piazza Matteotti, crossing the Via Cassia, and moving along Viale Colesanti with gigantic age-old plane trees on either side.

The lake, 13.5 km long and 12 km across, is the largest lake of volcanic origin in Europe. Hundreds of thousands of years ago, fractures were created in the recently formed lands and ashes, lapilli, pozzolana and lava were spewed out by explosions, emptying the underlying area so that the surface crust sank forming a *caldera*. In the course of tens of thousands of years this rain-collecting basin created the lake of Bolsena.

◄ Viale Colesanti

▼ The "rotunda at the lakeside avenue"

Volcanic activity continued and other explosions inside the lake led to the formation of two islands, Martana and Bisentina, now two dark green spots on the vast crystalline surface.

▲▼ Two charming pictures along the "lakeside avenue"

▲ The "small port" of Bolsena

► View of the lake and Isola Martana

Boats for public transportation can effectuate excursions on the lake and guided tours of the two islands, departing from the ports of Bolsena and Capodimonte.

ISOLA MARTANA

The island of *Martana* lies across from the town of Marta. Like the Isola Bisentina, it was a free commune in the

Middle Ages, and then followed the Papal fortunes.

With respect to the other island, Martana is harsher, but the landscape in certain parts of the year is particularly enchanting.

While it had a flourishing religious life in the Middle Ages, the island is known as the place where Amalasunta met her tragic fate. Daughter of Theodoric and queen of the Goths, when her father died, according to his dispositions, she took over the regency of the Ostrogothic kingdom for about nine years (526-535), since her son Atalaric was still too young.

Despite the fact that there were no precedents for the regency of a woman, and that it was Theodoric who had imposed Amalasunta, she is remembered in the sources as "learned and with a virile soul". She participated directly in the political activities of directing

the kingdom, re-established good relations with Byzantium and favored the Roman element.

When she fell out with the Ostrogoth nobles she was forced to divide the kingdom with her cousin Theodatus, by whom she was assassinated in 535.

Historical sources are not very clear as to just where Amalasunta was killed. In his *Gothic War (De bello Gothico)* Procopius of Caesarea tells us: "There is a lake in Tuscany, called Vulsinio, in which rises an island that is truly small but furnished with a strong castle. It was there that Theodatus kept Amalasunta prisoner". That island could also be Bisentina on which, at the time, there was a fortification, but a consolidated tradition, upheld by a majority, says that Martana was the fatal island of the Ostrogoth queen.

▼ The rock with the plaque in memory of the murder of Amalasunta

ISOLA BISENTINA

The *Bisentina* island lies facing the town of Capodimonte. Like nearby Martana, it is what remains of an ancient volcanic cone and owes its name to *Bisentium*, a flourishing center in Etruscan, Roman and medieval times that stood opposite.

It is the larger of the two islands, 700 meters long and 500 wide, and is a vast natural park with a flourishing vegetation, in particular holm oaks, and where many kinds of animals live.

Traces of pile dwellings, now under water off the island, are evidence that humans were already present on Bisentina in the archaic period. Finds of tombs and pottery dating to around the 6th century B.C. bear witness to settlements in Etruscan times. Like the Etruscans, the Romans too left traces of their stay on the island.

In the 9th century the populations of the towns along the shores took refuge there to escape the Saracen raids.

Around the middle of the 13th century it became the property of the lords of Bisenzio who, out of spite with regards to the island dwellers who did not support them in their struggles for domination of the lake, burned the island and abandoned it.

When Pope Urban IV was elected in 1261, he decided to restore papal prestige in the dominions of the Church, including the two islands in the lake.

▼ Bird's-eye view of Isola Bisentina

The pope reconquered the Bisentina island and, to cancel the memory of the past signoria of the Bisenzi, had it called Urbana after himself. The fortress the Bisenzi had razed to the ground was rebuilt. At the bottom of the tower a preceding excavation was used as prison and known as *della Malta* (that is *of mud*), where Angelario, abbot of Montecassino was imprisoned in 1295, as was Ranieri Ghiberti, Great Master of the Templars in 1299 and a group of heretical monks in 1359.

In 1296 Pope Boniface VIII subjugated the island to the dominion of Orvieto, although with reservations.

In 1333, it was destroyed by Louis of Bavaria, accused of heresy and excommunicated by the pope.

In 1400 the Isola Bisentina became the property of the Farnese. Around the middle of that year Ranuccio Farnese was buried there (a century later another Ranuccio Farnese, nephew of Paul III, was also buried there).

In 1462 the lord of Capodimonte Gabriele Farnese organized a historical regatta of fishermen from the lakeshore towns for Pope Pius II, Enea Silvio Piccolomini. After varying fortunes it was concluded with the victory of the Martani, to

the disgrace and humiliation of the Bolsenesi.

In October of 1517 Cardinal Alessandro Farnese organized a reception on the island in honor of Pope Leo X.

In the years around 1530 Cardinal Farnese, surrounded by scholars such as Paolo Giovio and Paolo Cortese, spent his summers on the island. In 1534 he was elected pope with the name of Paul III.

In 1635 the Isola Bisentina was governed by the duke of Castro Odoardo Farnese. He was in deep debt with the Monte di Pietà of Rome, putting up the duchy as warranty. Pope Urban VIII, already at logger-heads with the Farnese, took the pretext of this warranty to add the Duchy of Castro to the Ecclesiastical Dominions. France intervened in the struggle between the pope and the duke of Castro and the question was temporarily laid to rest. Innocent X brought his predecessor's project to fulfillment, with the total destruction of Castro in 1649.

With the end of the Duchy of Castro, both the islands, Martana and Bisentina, returned to the Church.

In 1707, under Pope Clement XI, the Apostolic Chamber conceded the use of Bisentina to the bishop of Montefiascone as a vacation spot for the Seminary of that diocese. This concession was confirmed until 1752, when the island was given in emphyteusis to Count Giraud, who transformed it into a park.

After changing hands various times, the island was bought in 1912 by Princess Beatrice Spada Potenziani, wife of Duke Fieschi Ravaschieri.

It is thanks to Prince Giovanni Fieschi Ravaschieri del Drago that after a long period of almost total abandon, the island is once more flourishing.

▲ The Renaissance Church of Santi
Giacomo e Cristoforo, by Vignola

◄ The Tempietto of Santa Caterina,
known as "la Rocchina",
attributed to Sangallo the Younger

It is open to the public and can be visited accompanied by a guide.

Monuments of note on the island include first of all the Renaissance *Church of Santi Giacomo e Cristoforo*, commissioned from Vignola by Cardinal Alessandro Farnese.

Scattered around the island are seven small chapels, the finest of which is the *Tempietto of Santa Caterina*, octagonal in plan, commonly called the *Rocchina*, attributed to Antonio da Sangallo the Younger. The oldest is the *Oratory of San Francesco*, while the *Oratory of Monte Oliveto*, dating to the early 17th century, probably replaced an older tempietto mentioned by Vasari.

The other Towns around the Lake

*T*he splendid towns that surround the lake can be visited in a ring itinerary.

Departing from Bolsena and taking the SS. Cassia in a southeast direction, after 15 km. one reaches Montefiascone from which a panoramic road winds through woods and fields to the lake front.

From Montefiascone, along the SP. Verentana, that once went to Vulci and then to the Tyrrhenian coast, one reaches the southern shore of the lake with Marta, Capodimonte and, further west, Valentano.

Continuing in a northwest direction, one arrives at the small towns of Gradoli and Grotte di Castro.

Leaving the last named, to return again to the SS. Cassia, one enters San Lorenzo Nuovo.

San Lorenzo Nuovo

Grotte di Castro

Bolsena

Gradoli

Isola Bisentina

Montefiascone

Isola Martana

Valentano

Capodimonte

Marta

▲ Panorama of Montefiascone

MONTEFIASCONE

Although Montefiascone does not lie on the shores of the lake, the fact that it stands on the highest hill of the Volsini mountains makes it the dominating landmark in the surrounding landscape. It is connected to the lake by a tortuous road that winds down the hill.

The town stands on the site of an Etruscan *pagus*, and may have been where the *Falisci* went after they were driven from *Faleri* by the Roman conquerors. It was therefore known as *Mons Faliscorum*, which then became Montefiascone.

The first historical information on the city dates to the Middle Ages, when the ham-

let that stood around the Church of San Flaviano was moved to the top of the hill in a more easily defended position after the sacking and plunder of the epoch of Barbarian invasions.

Montefiascone soon became part of the dominions of the Church, although it was organized as a free Commune. Alexander III indeed considered it his personal property and gave it to Giovanni de Vico in the 12th century. In 1240 it was subjugated by Frederick II and in 1252 fell under Ghibelline domination until it was securely returned to the Patrimony of the Church, and became the seat of the Rectors.

Urban IV chose it as his summer residence. Urban V bestowed Episcopal rank on the city.

After varying fortunes, including occupation by the most powerful families of the time, such as the Vico and the Sforza, in 1442 Montefiascone once more became a Church possession, hosting in the course of centuries illustrious personages, such as Clement VII who stopped there on his way to Orvieto, after being driven from Rome by the Lansquenets (1527), and the Emperor Charles V (1536).

The *Church of San Flaviano* is an interesting example of early Romanesque architecture (around the year thousand). It consists of two superimposed differently oriented churches, built almost one within the other, a lower and an upper church, characterized by a *matroneum* or women's gallery.

The lower church is the most interesting. Romanesque elements mix with typically Gothic ones. Of particular note are the capitals of the columns and piers on which the vault arches rest, the thirteenth-century baptismal font and the fifteenth- and sixteenth-century frescoes.

The facade, incomplete, has three Gothic arches and a loggetta dating to the 16th century, the columns of which are an eighteenth-century renovation.

The *Cathedral of Santa Margherita*, dedicated to the saint of Antioch, was erected at the end of the 15th century to a design by Michele Sanmicheli, but work continued until the 17th century with the construction of the imposing dome by Carlo Fontana.

The bell towers and the facade date to the middle of the 19th century. The Cathedral houses a canvas depicting the *Death*

▼ The Church of San Flaviano, interior *and* exterior

The Wine Fair of Montefiascone

Montefiascone is a town famous for its flourishing enological industry and its fine *Est! Est!! Est!!!* wines.

According to tradition the German baron Giovanni Defuk, perhaps a prelate in the following of Henry V, was so fond of fine wines that he entrusted a servant with the unusual task of marking the doors of the taverns where good wine was to be had with the word *Est* (it's here). His faithful man found a wine in

Montefiascone so exceptional that he marked it with *Est* three times. His master was delighted and drank so much that he died in 1113. He was buried in San Flaviano and on his tombstone are the words. EST! EST!! EST!!! PROPTER NIMIUM EST EST HIC JOANNES DE FUK DOMINUS MEUS MORTUS EST.

In memory of this event, halfway between legend and history, every year in Montefiascone in the first two weeks of August the traditional *Fiera del Vino* is held. This consists in a re-enactment of what happened, as well as being a pleasant occasion for tasting the local wine, semi-sweet and sparkling, with folkloristic and musical performances.

► The Papal Fort

of Saint Joseph, of the school of Sassoferrato (17th cent.) and a large altarpiece attributed to Benedetto Buglioni (15th cent.). The mortal remains of the saint who was martyred under Diocletian are preserved in the crypt.

The Rocca or Fort was built in 1262 by Urban IV who had chosen Montefiascone as his summer residence. During the Middle Ages it served as refuge and strategic base for the legates the popes sent from Avignon as Rectors of the Patrimony of Saint Peter. In the 13th century the Rocca became a real fortress and was further enlarged during the Renaissance.

Since the citizens of Montefiascone opposed Alessandro Farnese's attempt to incorporate the city in his dominions, when he became pope as Paul III, he removed the garrison as well as the cannons from the Fortress.

It began to fall into disrepair and was eventually semi-destroyed.

Recent restoration has once more made it available for cultural events and activities.

▼ The imposing dome of Santa Margherita, by Carlo Fontana

MARTA

Located on the southern shore of the lake, Marta stands next to the point where the river of the same name flows out of the lake. Tradition has it that Marta is located on an Etruscan settlement but the first certain mention of the town dates to the 10th century A.D.

It was part of the Patrimony of the Church, almost without interruption for centuries, with the exception of the periods in which it was subject to this or

▼ The clock Tower, an octagonal structure set on a square base

The traditional event of the *Barabbata* is a religious festival that is strongly folkloristic in its nature and of great anthropologic interest. It takes place on May 14th each year.

The roots are obviously pagan and can perhaps be traced back to the ancient propitiatory rites in honor of Ceres (Roman goddess of agriculture), adopted by Christianity and dedicated to Mary.

The origin of the name *Barabbata* is controversial. Some say it derives from the definition

that signoria: the Bisenzi, the Vico, the Orsini, the Farnese. It was with the last named that Marta became part of the Duchy

The Feast of the Modonna del Monte *"Barabbata"* of Marta

"things of Barabbas", that is a feast in which confusion, riotousness reign. The fact that the Bishop of Montefiascone once prohibited this festival on account of it's pagan overtones might corroborate this hypothesis. It was subsequently revived in a more sedate version. Others say that the name *Barabbata* derives from the fact that the rites begin late at night, and the *merry makers* seem to be wandering through the town as if they were "looking for Barabbas". Whatever the origin of the name, it is still a lovely and fascinating festival.

The ritual begins with the procession in which all the representatives of the professions and arts, bearing their symbols, the tools, the products of their work, are included. These are the *Casenghi*, the *Bifolchi*, the *Villani* and the *Pescatori*. The marvelously decorated floats, drawn by oxen or tractors, are laden with cheeses, barrels of wine, ripe harvests, fruits of every season preserved with particular techniques, and marvelous examples of the fish from the lake.

When the procession reaches the Church of the Madonna del Monte, Mass is celebrated, after which the *passate* take place, three rounds of the procession leaving from a secondary door of the church and re-entering by the main door, after which it returns to town, enthusiastically greeted by the inhabitants who throw broom-flower petals from the windows, while the *passanti* wear the traditional *ciambella* on their arms.

of Castro (1537), until that was destroyed (1649).

The landscape of Marta is dominated by a majestic square tower with an octagonal structure that, together with the gates and remains of the walls, is all that remains of the Fort

▲ Marta with Isola Martana
in the background

that Urban IV had built in the 13th century.

The Renaissance *Palazzo Farnese*, with its simple architectural lines, overlooks the main piazza.

Not far from the inhabited center, on a hill, is the small austere Romanesque *Church of the Madonna del Monte*, with an elegant Renaissance portal. The site is the point of arrival for the traditional *Barabbata*.

The inhabitants of Marta are renowned as fishermen, above all of eels, and as expert vintners who produce a limited quantity of *cannaiola*, the fine wine typical of this town on the lake.

▼ The remains
of the thirteenth-century fortress

▲ Panorama of Capodimonte

CAPODIMONTE

Not far from Marta, on the southern shore of the lake, Capodimonte lies up high on a steep peninsula that turns into a lava ridge.

Archaeological finds bear witness to Etruscan settlements on this small peninsula and probably Capodimonte is nothing but heir to the ancient *Bisentium* that was located nearby and was abandoned during the Barbarian invasions.

Earliest mention as *Castrum Capitis Montis* dates to the 12th century. The dominion of various lords, now one, now the other, were under the hegemony either of Orvieto or of the Church.

In 1315, when Capodimonte together with other lakeshore towns rebelled against the papal vicar, it was punished by exclusion but a few decades later it solemnly reconfirmed its loyalty to the Church.

As feud of the Farnese family, it hosted many illustrious personages: scholars, artists, prelates and popes, including Eugene IV, Alexander VI, Pius II, Julius II, Leo X and Gregory XIII.

When the Duchy of Castro, of which Capodimonte became part thanks to the Farnese, was razed to the ground by Innocent X, the town was reintegrated into the Patrimony of the Church.

The *Rocca*, a palace-fortress built by Pier Luigi Farnese between

▼ Typical view of the hamlet *and* panorama from the Fort

the end of the 15th and the early 16th century, dominates the landscape and serves as a reminder of the Farnese dominion. Designed by Antonio da Sangallo the Younger, the octagonal building was built on the square city walls and has an elegant facade in a typically Renaissance style.

Ancient necropoli, above all in località Piana di San Bernardino and Bucacce, have *pozzetto tombs* of Villanovan date, Etruscan *chamber* and *fossa tombs* and large Roman *colombaria*. The countless archaeological finds, including the typical and famous Etruscan *hinged sandals*, are now in various Italian and foreign museums.

▲ The Church of San Rocco

▼ A captivating image of the "Luminata"

The landscape of Capodimonte is particularly picturesque with the houses perched on the small lava promontory, the long sandy beach and the tree-shaded promenade.

The economy of the town is mostly tourism, a popular place in summer, but fishing and agriculture are also important.

For the feast of Saint Roch, patron saint of the town, in the middle of August, the characteristic *Luminata* takes place in Capodimonte. The procession starts in the Collegiata of Santa Maria Assunta, winds through the streets to the Church of San Rocco while the sky is filled with fireworks and decked out and illuminated boats pass by on the lake.

VALENTANO

Valentano is higher up (538 m.) on one of the Volsini hills on the southwest side of the lake, with a sweeping view of the fertile plain up to the Apennines.

The territory of Valentano is particularly interesting from a naturalistic point of view, with cultivated fields, woods that change color and appearance with the seasons, the fascinating quarries of red lapillus that lend the landscape a surreal aspect.

The origins of Valentano may go far back, as some affirm, all the way to the Etruscan *Verentum*. The first historical mention however dates to the medieval period and some historians maintain that the town was built in 1053 for Pope Leo IX. From then on Valentano was subjugated now to the Church, now to Viterbo, now to Orvieto, in the cycle of struggles for predominion over the lake. This continued until 1262 when Urban IV reintegrated it into the papal domains.

Between 1254 and 1350 Valentano was repeatedly plundered and destroyed, and in 1328 the army of Louis of Bavaria razed it to the ground.

▼ Panorama of Valentano

▶ The sixteenth-century Town Hall

The town was completely rebuilt, thanks to the fact that the Church exonerated it from taxes.

Like all other centers that lie along the shores of the lake, Valentano too, at a certain point, became a Farnese dominion. In the middle of the 14th century Pope Innocent VI gave the town to the Farnese, a domination that lasted until the Duchy of Castro came to an end.

The principal landmark of

Valentano is an old *Fortress* built by the Farnese on an earlier building that had already been renovated more than once. Various details of the inner courtyard would seem to indicate that it was designed by Antonio da Sangallo the Younger. The castle has been splendidly restored and is in part used for cultural activities (east wing) and the **Library** and the **Museum of the Prehistory of Tuscia and the Farnese Fortress** are located here.

The inhabitants of Valentano are above all farmers, growing grain and grapes. The traditional *Tiratura del solco diritto* is held every August 15th in honor of the land. The most skilful farmers, with a plow (once pulled by oxen) trace a furrow about five kilometers long on the *piana* or level tract of land. The straighter the furrow, the more abundant the harvest.

GRADOLI

The pleasant town of Gradoli is located in a stupendous panoramic site northwest of the lake, on the inner slopes of the Volsinii mountains. It has a mild climate and Pope Paul III even said that those who wished to live forever should spend the summer in Gradoli and the winter in Canino…

Numerous traces remain of ancient Roman settlements. In the Middle Ages it was a free Commune, and was invaded more than once, first by the troops of Louis of Bavaria (1328), then by the Bretons (1394).

Around the middle of the 15th century, after varying fortunes, it passed under the Farnese and was included in the Duchy of Castro in 1537. When this fell (1649) it returned to the Patrimony of the Church.

The heart of the town consists of the medieval quarter entered through an old gate. It is dominated by the imposing yet aerial edifice of the *Palazzo Farnese*, built to designs by Antonio da Sangallo the Younger, on the foundations of an older castle documented from 1118 on. The Palace, with its exquisite and elegant Renaissance forms, is outstanding and contains fireplaces in peperino, splendid coffered wooden ceilings and frescoes by the Zuccari (16th cent.). After a long and careful restoration the building is now as splendid as it once was and houses the *Town Hall*, a **Museum of Ceramics** of the 15th and 16th century (with material found in a "*butto*" or palace dump in

▼ Palazzo Farnese *and* the Church of Santa Maria Maddalena

▲ The complex of the Church of Santa Maria Maddalena and Palazzo Farnese

1980), the **Municipal Historical Archives** with sixteenth- to nineteenth-century documents, a **Section of Renaissance Costumes** and a **Centro Studi Farnesiani e di Richerche sul Territorio**.

The *Church of Santa Maria Maddalena* stands next to the Palazzo Farnese. Inside is a marble baptismal font attributed to the school of Donatello (15th cent.). The bell tower is 18th century.

The *Church of San Magno* is in the territory of the municipality of Gradoli, but on the shores of the lake. With fine fifteenth-century lines, it was given by the Farnese to the Knights of Malta and was redeemed by the Municipality of Gradoli in 1896.

The Gradoli coat of arms contains a grapevine and a rampant lion. The grapevine is the symbol of the typical wine of Gradoli, *aleatico*, with a decided fragrant flavor, known world wide, and *grechetto*, with a mellow flavor and a high alcoholic content.

► The Church of San Magno

The Purgatory Dinner
of Gradoli

An ancient tradition is renewed every year in Gradoli. The origins go back to times in which the *Fratellanza del Purgatorio*, a brotherhood that still exists, collected suffrages for the souls in purgatory.

The event takes place in two distinctly different moments: Holy Thursday and Ash Wednesday.

On Thursday, a procession of hooded figures moves through the lanes of the town collecting gifts in kind (oil, wine, cheese, sausages...) that will be auctioned off that same day. The money collected is then used for the characteristic *Dinner of Purgatory*, in which around two thousand persons generally take part.

The fortunate guests, paying a sum that is on the whole symbolic, enjoy a truly delicious Lenten meal in which the following are served: cannellini beans (known as *of Purgatory*) seasoned with the excellent local olive oil, fish soup with rice, lake fish stewed or fried, cod, all washed down of course with glasses of the famous local wines.

▲▼ Panorama of Grotte di Castro *and* an Etruscan tomb in the necropolis of Pianezze

GROTTE DI CASTRO

G rotte di Castro stands on a tufa outcropping of the Volsini mountains, on the northwest side of the lake.

The town seems to have been built on an earlier Etruscan settlement that was destroyed in 280 B.C. by the Romans. An Etruscan *polis* apparently stood on the hill of the Roman *Civita* that local tradition indicates as Tyro.

In the 7th century the city was destroyed by the Lombards and then by the Saracens. After the Saracen raids the inhabitants of the area took refuge in the ancient tombs and natural caves, which gave rise to the name *Castrum Cryp-*

tarum, later transformed into Grotte di Castro.

In the early Middle Ages the small center was long con-

◄ The Town Hall

known as *Cento Camere, Vigna della Piazza* and *Le Sane*, in the midst of fascinating natural surroundings, can in part be visited.

The *Basilica* dedicated to *Maria SS. del Suffragio* was built in 1625 on an earlier eighth-century structure. The small museum in the vaults contains sacred objects and vestments and interesting Etruscan finds.

At the center of the town is the *Church of San Pietro Apostolo*, built by Matilde of Canossa around the year 1000. Repeatedly destroyed by fire, all that remains of the original Romanesque structure is the bell tower.

The *Town Hall*, with its fine spiral staircase in stone, was built in the 16th century to plans by Vignola. Of note also is the imposing *Palazzo of Innocenzo Iuzzi* of 1563.

The **Museo Civico Archeologico e delle Tradizioni Popolari** (entrance on Via del Fede) is located in the former *Palazzo del Podestà*. It has an Etruscan and a medieval section.

tended for by Sovana, Orvieto and Acquapendente, each of which claimed the right of jurisdiction, until this right was conceded first to the diocese of Orvieto, then to that of Montefiascone. Subsequently Grotte di Castro passed to the various signorias: the Vico, Orsini, Tartaglia, until it was subjugated to the Farnese when the Duchy of Castro was constituted (1537), later to return to the Patrimony of the Church.

Vestiges of the numerous necropoli scattered throughout its territory bear witness to the Etruscan origins of Grotte. Of particular interest are the approximately 250 Etruscan hypogeum composite chamber tombs of *Pianezze*, currently being restored. The necropoli

Every ten years a solemn religious event in honor of the Madonna del Suffragio takes place in the first decade of September. The image of the Virgin, kept covered in the years before the feast, is shown to the faithful who carry her in procession through the streets of the town, decked out and sprinkled with flowers.

The economy of the small town is based exclusively on agriculture. The potatoes of Grotte di Castro are particularly renowned and are celebrated every year in the middle of August in the *Sagra della Patata* where visitors can enjoy a series of tasty dishes.

▼ Two pictures of the Basilica-Shrine of Maria SS. del Suffragio

▲ San Lorenzo Nuovo,
the octagonal piazza overlooked
by the Church of San Lorenzo Martire

SAN LORENZO NUOVO

▼ Church of San Lorenzo Martire,
twelfth-century *wooden Crucifix*

Located on the western edge of the Volsini mountains, San Lorenzo Nuovo dominates the entire basin of the lake, up to Monte Amiata. The center is called *Nuovo* or New because it replaced the "old", located further down in an area near the lake and unhealthy because of the marshes where hemp was macerated. Around the middle of the 18th century an epidemic of malaria reduced the population of the old San Lorenzo to a few hundred souls. A new town therefore had to be built for the survivors of the old center and in only four years (1774-1778) San Lorenzo Nuovo, a perfect example of an eighteenth-century town plan, was built in a healthier site.

The new settlement, designed by the architect Francesco Navone, has an octagonal layout with the neoclassic *Church of San Lorenzo Martire* on one side. The piazza is crossed, north-south, by the Via Cassia that, in turn, is intersected at right angles by another wide street from which a network of smaller streets moves out in parallel and perpendicular lines.

Inside the church are a thirteenth-century *wooden Crucifix*, two canvases by Vasari and the *marble bust of Pius VI*, attributed to the school of Canova.

Caves with the characteristic Roman *colombaria* are found in the environs of the old San Lorenzo.

The history of the town is quite like that of the other towns around the lake. From 1100 on it was almost continuously a dominion of the Church, except for the period from 1265 to 1359 in which it was under the Commune of Orvieto.

The inhabitants of San Lorenzo Nuovo are principally farmers and tradesmen. The potato is one of the prevalent crops. And it is in honor of this tasty tuber that the *Sagra degli Gnocchi,* a relatively recent festival, takes place in the days before Ferragosto. Participants can enjoy the exquisite gnocchi in sauce as they listen to concerts, all in the central square. The livestock fair and market on the Feast day of St. John on June 24th is a traditional appointment for locals and visitors alike. Around ten in the morning, after roaming through the streets with stands of all kinds, the visitor can buy pickled eels and porchetta and enjoy them together with a bottle of *aleatico* in one of the wine cellars open for the occasion.

▼ Church of San Lorenzo Martire, *marble bust of Pius VI*, school of Canova

Pastimes and good food

The water of the lake of Bolsena, now particularly clear and limpid thanks to an imposing sophisticated purification system managed by a consortium of Communes of the lake basin (CO.BA.L.B.), and to the fact that there are no pollution-generating industries in the area, has always been clean.

The mild climate is particularly suited to children and older people.

Bolsena and the other towns along the lake have created efficient tourist facilities for those who come to enjoy the splendid uncontaminated natural environment. Many campsites, located above all in Bolsena, Montefiascone and Capodimonte, host foreign and Italian visitors, many of whom come back year after year. All camp sites are equipped with modern and adequate facilities, but some are truly avant-garde in the criteria with which they have been planned: masonry bungalows, trailers, sport facilities, markets, hot and cold showers, restaurants and pizza parlors.

Bolsena also has a number of qualified hotels, fully equipped with modern facilities, many of which overlook the lake. For those who prefer to stay in houses and apartments, even for short periods, there are specific real estate agencies. The sports that

an be practiced on the lake include sailing, motor boating, water skiing and windsurfing. fishing, in the limits established by the law, is also permitted.

Bicycle paths along the avenues and lakeshore boulevards have level and shaded itineraries for the cyclist.

Restaurants, trattorias, pubs and pizza parlors galore offer the gastronomic delicacies of the area.

When speaking of eating and drinking on the shores of the lake of Bolsena, place of honor goes to the sweetwater fish, prized and tasty, famous from ancient times: eels, whitefish, perch, tench, pike, whitebait, mullet among others. Paolo Giovio who stayed on the Bisentina island in Alessandro Farnese's court praised them in his *Trattato dei pesci*. But Dante had preceded him when, in his *Purgatory*, referring to the gluttonous Martin IV, he wrote: "...and by his fasting purges Bolsena eels, and good Vernaccia wine." (canto XXIV, 23/24).

The typical dish of the fishermen of the lake of Bolsena, to be found in specialized trattorias, is the *sbroscia*, a fish stew in which chunks of tench, pike, eel, perch (whitefish and whitebait can be added when the stew is almost done since they are

the tenderest of all), together with slices of potato, onion and pennyroyal, seasoned with olive oil, salt and chili pepper. When done the *sbroscia* is served on slices of day-old or toasted bread.

The delicate flavorful perch is usually filleted and cooked *alla mugnaia* or fried. The whitefish is served grilled or boiled with sauce of some kind.

The fresh vegetables that thrive around the lake are used in summer for tasty minestrones of zucchini, freshly hulled beans, celery, carrots, chard, savoy cabbage, green beans and ripe tomatoes. Or the vegetables can be eaten in *pinzimonio* (dipped raw in oil, lemon juice, salt and pep-

per) or, mixed with aromatic wild herbs in fresh salads.

In winter the local cuisine gives preference to dry legumes: beans, lentils, chick peas and fava beans that, together with the pasta, supply flavorful nourishing one-dish meals, ideal for those who follow a Mediterranean diet.

Speaking of pasta…! The housewives of Tuscia almost always make it at home by hand. From the *lombrichelli*, to potato gnocchi, *fettucine* and *pappardelle*, all eaten with a rich meat sauce and grated pecorino cheese.

The fish may be the lords of our table, but meat too has a place of primary importance, above all pork, processed and cooked in a thousand different ways: sausages, chops, ribs, liver, prosciutto and the typical *porchetta*, seasoned with wild fennel. Lamb is popular too: roasted, *scottadito* (grilled chops) and in stews. Appetizers generally consist

of assorted locally produced salted meats such as *coppa, lonza, lombetto* and *prosciutto*, of variously seasoned *bruschette* - with garlic, oil and salt, with tomatoes and basil, with a liver paste, with olive and artichoke pastes, etc.

Some of the commonly served desserts in the area are also home-made and unique such as the *tozzetti* and the *maccheroni con le noci*, a sweet that also serves as first course on Christmas eve, the fragrant Easter cakes and the rice fritters, typical of the feast of Saint Joseph.

Naturally every typical dish has to be accompanied by a local wine, from the *Est! Est!! Est!!!* of Montefiascone, dry and semi-sweet, to the robust wines that come from the union of various types of grapes that prosper on the slopes of the Volsini hills, ranging from the red *cannaiola* of Marta to the aromatic sweeter *aleatico* of Gradoli.

Day outings

*A*nyone who stops in Bolsena for tourism, can take interesting outings *every day, into both the upper area of Viterbo and as far as Umbria and Tuscany.*

Viterbo ➡ Bagnaia ➡ ➡ La Quercia ➡ Ferento ➡ ➡ Caprarola

*O*nly 30 kilometers from Bolsena, following the state highway Cassia south, is **Viterbo**, the capital of the province. The City of the Popes is particularly famous as the place where various popes stayed in the Middle Ages, choosing it as the seat for the conclaves for the election of a new pope.

Viterbo is embraced by powerful towered walls erected between the 12th and 13th century. At its heart is the medieval quarter of *San Pellegrino* characterized by fine *profferli* (external staircase out-side many houses) and *coats of arms* on the corners of the buildings. Of particular artistic note are the *Town Hall* (15th cent.), the *Cathedral of San Lorenzo* (12th cent. with a 16th cent. facade), the *Papal Palace* (13th cent.), with the stupendous crenellated facade and its two-light openings, the *Church of Santa Maria della Verità* (12th cent.), with the annexed **Museo Civico**, the *Churches of Santa Maria Nuova* and *of San Sisto*, both with structures dating to the 9th century, the *Church of San Francesco*, Gothic with a Romanesque portal, and the *Shrine of Santa Rosa*, patron saint of the city.

Leaving Viterbo in a south-

▶ *Viterbo*, the Cathedral

▲ *Viterbo*, the Palace of the Popes

east direction, after a couple of kilometers along a tree-shaded avenue, one reaches La Quercia, a hamlet of Viterbo, with the *Shrine of the Madonna della Quercia* (15th-16th cent.), an elegant Renaissance church with an austere facade and a fine coffered ceiling.

Continuing, one reaches **Bagnaia**, also a hamlet of Viterbo,

five kilometers from the city. It is famous for the splendid ***Villa Lante***, built between the 15th and 16th century for the cardinals Riario, Gambara and Montalto, while the name is derived from the Lante della Rovere family that took it over in the 17th century. For some years now the Villa has belonged to the Italian State.

The complex of Villa Lante, designed by Vignola, consists of two small symmetrical buildings with a three-arched loggia on the ground floor and a belvedere on the roof. Entrance is through a stupendous Italian-style garden that broadens into a large square at the center of which is the *Fountain of the Four Moors*. The garden

◄ *La Quercia*,
the Shrine of the Madonna della Quercia

◀▲ *Bagnaia*, bird's eye view of the "borgo" and Villa Lante *and* the Palazzina Gambara

rises in five superposed levels with fountains and jets of water one after the other in the midst of a luxuriant green vegetation.

Returning to Viterbo and this time leaving in a northeast direction, after about eight kilometers are the ruins of the ancient **Ferento**, a city that flourished in Imperial Roman as well as Etruscan times.

The entire archaeological zone is of interest, but the *Ro-*

▼ *Ferento*, the Roman Theater

▲ *Caprarola*, Palazzo Farnese *and* the splendid Scala Regia

man Theater is the most important. For years now performances of various kinds have been presented here during the summer: symphonic concerts, operas, ballet, and plays both modern and ancient.

Eighteen kilometers south-east of Viterbo, on an elevation in the Cimini mountains, is **Caprarola**, famous for its imposing *Palazzo Farnese* (second half 16th cent.), one of the most significant architectural complexes of Italian Mannerism. It was built by Vignola (1507-1573) on the foundations of a pentagonal fort designed for Paul III by Antonio da Sangallo the Younger.

The palace, with a tall five-story facade, adapts to the rise in the land with a double two-ramp staircase and is impressive in its severity thanks to the five bastions at the corners. Inside, the spiral *Scala Regia* leads to the upper rooms with frescoes by the Zuccari (16th cent.) as well as fine furnishings and decorations of the late 16th century.

Tuscania ➡️
➡️ Tarquinia ➡️ Vulci

Leaving Bolsena for Montefiascone and continuing to Marta, one reaches **Tuscania** (50 km.), a town famous for the *Basilicas of San Pietro* and *Santa Maria Maggiore*, both splendid examples of architecture that straddles Early Christian and early Romanesque styles (8th-9th cent.). Tuscania preserves numerous signs of its Etruscan and Roman past, including the ruins of a city wall, baths and a necropolis.

▲ *Tuscania*, the Basilicas of San Pietro *and* of Santa Maria Maggiore

About 25 kilometers from Tuscania is **Tarquinia**. It was of great importance in Etruscan times and exercised a strong influence on Rome, to which it gave the dynasty of the Tar-quins. The many tombs dug into the tufa remain as evidence of this flourishing pe-

▲ *Tarquinia*, bird's eye view *and* the famous *Winged Horses* in the Museo Nazionale Etrusco

riod. Their wall paintings furnish us with the best examples of Etruscan figural art. Numerous finds of inestimable historical and artistic value can be seen in the ***Museo Nazionale Etrusco***.

Leaving Tarquinia and taking the state highway Aurelia one reaches **Vulci**. With Bolsena as the point of departure, the same itinerary can be followed passing through Valentano and Canino. To be seen in Vulci is the old Abbey Castle (9th cent.), perched on a rocky ridge overlooking the gorges eaten out by the Fiora River below. To get to the castle one crosses the fascinating hump-backed Abbadia bridge, with Etruscan-Roman foundations. The castle now is the seat of the ***Museo Archeologico Nazionale*** with Etruscan finds from the 9th to the 3rd century B.C.: *bronzes, sculpture, pottery, inscriptions* and *ex-votos*. Not far off is the necropolis.

▲ *Vulci*, Castle and bridge of the Abbadia

Civita di Bagnoregio ➡ ➡ Orvieto

After leaving Bolsena on the Via Orvietana, at a certain point the road branches towards Civita di Bagnoregio (18 km.) on the right and Orvieto (18 km.) on the left.

Civita di Bagnoregio, known as *"la città che muore"* or *the dying city*, was once the original heart of Bagnoregio to which it was joined. A continuous and

▼ *Civita di Bagnoregio*

▼ *Orvieto*, the Gothic facade of the Cathedral and the *Chapel of San Brizio* inside

inexorable process of erosion ate away the tufa walls resting on clay and in the course of the centuries the two were separated by a great ravine. Civita remained isolated in the center of a valley surrounded by the characteristic *calanchi* or badlands. Today it can be reached by crossing an unusual 300 meter-long bridge. Once there, vestiges of its noble past are to be found in the *Palazzo Mazzocchi Alemanni* and the *Parish church of San Donato*.

Orvieto, in Umbria, also stands on a tufa cliff and its origins go far back in time. It can probably be identified with the Etruscan *Volsinii Veteres* and many interesting vestiges bear witness to this period, including the *Necropolis of Crocifisso del Tufo*, various tombs and temples.

The *Basilica of Saints Andrea and Bartolomeo* and the *Abbey of Saints Severo and Martirio* date to the early Middle Ages. In its original structures the *Church of San Giovenale* also goes back to a period prior to the 10th century. Orvieto flourished in medieval times and the town is characterized by numerous tower houses. Of particular interest is the *Palazzo del Popolo* (12th-13th cent.).

But it is the *Cathedral* that outshines all the other buildings. Illustrious artists were employed on this extraordinary beautiful piece of architecture from the 13th to the late 16th century, ranging from Arnolfo di Cambio, who may have prepared the original plan in Romanesque forms, to Lorenzo Maitani, who completed it and designed the richly Gothic facade, from Andrea Pisano to Orcagna, Ippolito Scalza to Raf-

faello da Montelupo. Inside the Cathedral is the marvelous *Chapel of San Brizio* with frescoes by Fra Angelico and above all Luca Signorelli (15th-16th cent.). The frescoes in the apse are by Ugolino di Prete Ilario (14th cent.). Other works include a fresco by Gentile da Fabriano and a *Reliquary* by Ugolino di Vieri (14th cent.).

Orvieto is also famous for *St. Patrick's Well*, built in the 16th century by Antonio da Sangallo the Younger, to ensure water to the city in case of siege.

Sovana ➡ Saturnia

Another day outing could be made touching the southernmost point of Tuscany, to **Sovana**. The town, only 40 kilometers from Bolsena, was an Etruscan center (to which

▶ *Sovana*, the Tomba Ildebranda

▲ *Sovana*, Piazza del Pretorio

the necropolis with 4th-3rd century tombs bear witness), and then a Roman center. Hildebrand of Sovana, future Pope Gregory VII was born here in the 11th century. To see in Sovana: the *Cathedral of Saints Peter and Paul* (12th-13th cent.), built on an earlier church, the *Church of Santa Maria* (12th-14th cent.), the thirteenth-century *Palazzo Pretorio*, renovated in the 15th century and later, and the ruins of the *Aldobrandesca Fortress or Rocca* (13th-14th cent.).

Saturnia, famous for its spa facilities, is also located in Tuscany, in the town of Manciano. It was an important Etruscan city and parts of the wall in polygonal work and the necropolis with single chamber tombs, are still extant.

◄ *Saturnia*,
hot water sulfur springs

PLEASE NOTE

The addresses and items listed are the result of a free selection by the editorial staff. This is in no way prejudicial regarding those not mentioned in this section of the guidebook. The Publishing House is not responsible for whatever variations there may be of telephone numbers, hours and names that may have changed after the date of publication.

HOW TO GET THERE

– The Lake of Bolsena is located in the region of Lazio (central Italy). The National and International Airport of Rome, Fiumicino, is around 140 kilometers away, while the port of Civitavecchia is around 40 kilometers from the first towns in the basin.

– For those coming from the Autostrada del Sole A1, exit at Orvieto, head for Viterbo and after around 10 kilometers, on the right, follow the indications for Bolsena.

– For those coming from Rome on the SS. Cassia in direction north, the first town on the lake to be encountered, 100 km. from the capital, will be Montefiascone.

– Arriving from the north along the SS. Cassia, after around 100 km. from Siena, one enters San Lorenzo Nuovo.

– On the Via Aurelia running along the Tyrrhenian Sea, whether coming from the north (Genoa, Livorno, Grosseto) or the south (Rome, Civitavecchia, Tarquinia), the best exit is Montalto di Castro, after which follow the indications for Canino and Valentano.

USEFUL NUMBERS

CARABINIERI) 112
FIRST AID EMERGENCY) 118
FINANCIAL POLICE) 117
NAVIGAZIONE TURISTICA ALTOLAZIO (Bolsena)) 0761/798033
NAVIGAZIONE TURISTICA LA BUSSOLA (Capodimonte)) 0761/870760
STATE POLICE – Public emergency assistance) 113
MARITIME RESCUE) 1530
FIRE DEPARTMENT) 115

Bolsena

CARABINIERI) 0761/799002
CATACOMBS OF SANTA CRISTINA)▣ 0761/799067
☺ winter: 9-11.30 a.m./3-5 p.m.
☺ summer: 9-11.30 a.m./3-6:30 p.m.
TOWN HALL) 0761/795412
CONSORZIO BACINO LAGO DI BOLSENA) 0761/799778
MUSEO TERRITORIALE DEL LAGO DI BOLSENA) 0761/798630
☺ winter: from Tuesdays to Fridays: 10 a.m.-1 p.m.; Satudays, Sundays and holidays: 10 a.m.-1 p.m./ 3-6 p.m.
☺ summer: 10 a.m.- 1 p.m./ 4-7:30 p.m.
Closed Mondays
ARCHAEOLOGICAL EXCAVATIONS (Scavi Archeologici) POGGIO MOSCINI
☺ open every day, including holidays: 8 a.m.-1:30 p.m.
Closed Mondays, January 1, May 1, December 25
TOURIST INFORMATION BUREAU
Piazza Matteotti, 12) 0761/799923
POST OFFICE) 0761/799018
MUNICIPAL POLICE) 0761/798771

Montefiascone

CARABINIERI) 0761/831056
TOWN HALL) 0761/83201
TOWN HALL - tourist information) 0761/820884
HOSPITAL) 0761/820600
HOSPITAL – FIRST AID) 0761/8331
PUBLIC TELEPHONES) 0761/826051
TOURIST INFORMATION OFFICE) 0761/832060
POST OFFICE) 0761/824177
MUNICIPAL POLICE) 0761/826789

Marta

CARABINIERI) 0761/870423
TOWN HALL) 0761/871531
CONFRATERNITA DELLA MISERICORDIA) 0761/872444
MUNICIPAL POLICE) 0761/871597
PUBLIC TELEPHONES) 0761/870856/871580
POST OFFICE) 0761/872220

Capodimonte
CARABINIERI) 0761/870042
TOWN HALL) 0761/870043
MUNICIPAL POLICE) 0761/872378
PUBLIC TELEPONES 0761/870030
POST OFFICE) 0761/870741

Valentano
CARABINIERI) 0761/422602
TOWN HALL) 0761/453001
RED CROSS - AMBULANCE
) 338.2611063
FIRST AID STATION) 0761/453453
MUSEO DELLA PREISTORIA DELLA
TUSCIA E DELLA ROCCA FARNESE
) 🖥 0761/420018
☼ winter:
Tuesdays to Fridays: 10 a.m.-1 p.m.
Saturdays: 10 a.m.-1 p.m./3-6 p.m.
Sundays: 10 a.m.-1 p.m.
Closed Mondays
☼ summer: from Wednesdays
to Fridays: 4-7 p.m.;
Saturdays and Sundays:
10 a.m.-1 p.m./4-7 p.m.:
Sundays: 10 a.m.-1 p.m.
Closed Mondays and Tuesdays
Closed on national holidays
PUBLIC TELEPHONES) 0761/422239
POST OFFICE) 0761/422272

Gradoli
CARABINIERI) 0761/456081
TOWN HALL) 0761/456082
MUSEO DEL COSTUME FARNESIANO
c/o Palazzo Farnese di Gradoli
(3º-4º floor)) 🖥 0761/456052
☼ winter: from Tuesdays
to Fridays: 10 a.m.-1 p.m.;
Saturdays: 10 a.m.-1 p.m./ 3-6 p.m.;
Sundays: 10 a.m.-1 p.m.
Closed Mondays
☼ summer: Wednesdays: 5-7 p.m.;
Thursdays: 11 a.m.-1 p.m./ 5-7 p.m.;
from Friday
to Sunday: 10 a.m.-1 p.m./5-7 p.m.;
on August 15th, open only on prior
reservation
Closed Mondays and Tuesdays
Closed January 1, April 25, May 1
MUNICIPAL POLICE) 0761/456703
PUBLIC TELEPHONES) 0761/456095
POST OFFICE) 0761/456083

Grotte di Castro
CARABINIERI) 0763/796002
TOWN HALL) 0763/798002
MUSEO CIVICO E DELLE TRADIZIONI
POPOLARI) 🖥 0763/797173
from January 10 to February 28:
from Mondays to Fridays visits on
prior reservation;
Saturdays-Sundays: 10:30 a.m.-4 p.m.
from March 1 to April 30:
from Mondays to Fridays visits
on prior reservation;
from March 1 to April 30: from Mondays
to Fridays visits on prior reservation;
Saturdays-Sundays: 10 a.m./3-6 p.m.
from May 1 to September 30: from
Tuesdays to Fridays: 4-7 p.m.;
Saturdays-Sundays: 10 a.m.-
12:30/4-7:30 p.m.
Closed Mondays, January 1, Easter,
December 25
PUBLIC TELEPHONES) 0763/796043
POST OFFICE) 0763/796033
TOURIST INFORMATION
) 0763/796966

San Lorenzo Nuovo
CARABINIERI) 0763/726177
TOWN HALL) 0763/727391
PUBLIC TELEPHONES) 0763/727051
POST OFFICE) 0763/727015

HOTELS
Bolsena
AI PLATANI ✱ ✱ ✱
Via Roma, 2
) 0761/799079-798787
🖥 0761/798468
COLUMBUS HOTEL SUL LAGO ✱ ✱ ✱
Viale Colesanti, 27
) 0761/799009 🖥 0761/798172
EDEN ✱ ✱ ✱
km 114.4 on the Cassia,
Loc. Tempietto, 46
) 0761/799015 🖥 0761/796343
ITALIA ✱
Corso Cavour, 53) 0761/799193
LE NAIADI SUL LAGO ✱ ✱ ✱
Viale Cadorna, 95
) 0761/799017 🖥 0761/798538
LIDO ✱ ✱ ✱
km 114.8 on the Cassia
) 0761/799026 🖥 0761/798479

LORIANA 1 e 2 SUL LAGO ✳ ✳ ✳
Viale Cadorna, 33
☎ 0761/799272 📠 0761/799273
NAZIONALE ✳ ✳ ✳
Via Gramsci, 50
☎ 0761/799006 📠 0761/799378
ROYAL ✳ ✳ ✳ ✳
Piazzale D. Alighieri, 8/10
☎ 0761/797048-9 📠 0761/796000
ZODIACO ✳ ✳ ✳
Via IV Novembre, 8
☎ 📠 0761/798791

Montefiascone
ALTAVILLA ✳ ✳ ✳
Via del Pino, 9
☎ 0761/826414 📠 0761/820123
CAMINETTO ✳ ✳
km. 102 on the Cassia ☎ 0761/826486
DANTE ✳ ✳
Via Nazionale, 2 ☎ 0761/826015
ITALIA & LOMBARDI ✳ ✳ ✳
Piazzale Roma, 9
☎ 0761/826058 📠 0761/831091
LA CARROZZA D'ORO
SUL LAGO ✳ ✳ ✳
Lungolago, 95
☎ 0761/823157 📠 0761/820211
RONDINELLA ✳ ✳
km 99.8 on the Cassia
☎ 📠 0761/824995

Marta
DA OTELLO ✳ ✳
Via Laertina, 5 ☎ 0761/871627

Capodimonte
RIVA BLU ✳ ✳
Via dei Pini, 3 ☎ 0761/870255

Valentano
PICCOLO HOTEL LA CIOTOLA ✳
Via della Villa, 27 ☎ 0761/422132

Gradoli
LA RIPETTA ✳ ✳ ✳
Via Roma, 38
☎ 0761/456100 📠 0761/456817

San Lorenzo Nuovo
ITALIA ✳
Via L. Turchetti, 3
☎ 0763/726040

STELLA SUL LAGO ✳ ✳
Loc. Prati Renari
☎ 📠 0763/727484

FARM HOLIDAY CENTERS
Bolsena
ANTICA FATTORIA
Loc. Casaletto
Str. Cassia km. 109.8
☎ 0761/799166
BELVEDERE
Via Belvedere, 104
☎ 0761/798290
LA FRASCHETTA
Str. Cassia Nord, 148
☎ 0761/799678
LA PIANTATA
Str. Cassia Nord, 58/a
☎ 0761/799794
LE PALME
Loc. Mezzagnone
Str. Cassia Nord km. 118
☎ 0761/799671-335/6199908
MONTEBELLO
Strada Orvietana km. 3
☎ 0761/799492 📠 0761/798965
PODERACCIO
Loc. Poderaccio, 76
☎ 0761/799594-798443

Valentano
FRA' VIACO
Via A. Gramsci, 52
☎ 0761/422070 📠 0761/420226
MONTE ROIO
Str. Prov.le Lago di Mezzano, 14
☎ 0761/453791 📠 0761/453142

Grotte di Castro
CASTELLO DI S.CRISTINA
Loc. Castello S. Cristina
☎ 📠 0763/78011
MONTEPERETO
Loc. Montepereto, 37
☎ 0763/796593 📠 0761/733642

San Lorenzo Nuovo
LA PALOMBARA
Loc. La Palombara, 19
☎ 0763/727588
LA SPINETTA
Loc. Spinetta
☎ 0763/779003

BED & BREAKFAST
Bolsena
AL CASTELLO
Via del Castello, 11
❱ 🖷 0761/799534-328/8662263
LE VIGNE
Via delle Vigne, 157b
❱ 🖷 0761/799875-347/8840312
TARA
Via Cassia, 9 - Loc. Feliciangelo
❱ 0761/799278

Marta
DELLA CANNARA
Via di Tuscania
❱ 🖷 0761/872121
LE PIETRE
Strada Campo le Rose, 2
❱ 🖷 0761/251900

Capodimonte
OLMO BELLO
Via Verentana, 60
❱ 0761/872365
TERESA AL LAGO
Via Puniatoschi, 12
❱ 0761/870287-347/8302490

Grotte di Castro
MAGI TURIST
Via Nobile, 19
❱ 0761/341974-347/3440783

CAMP SITES
Bolsena
BLU INTERNATIONAL CAMPING
km. 111.6 on the Cassia
on the Lake of Bolsena
❱ 🖷 0761/798855
CAPPELLETTA
km. 116.5 on the Cassia
(from Bolsena km. 3.5)
❱ 🖷 0761/799543
IL LAGO INTERNATIONAL
Viale Cadorna, 6
❱ 🖷 0761/799191
MASSIMO
km. 116.7 on the Cassia
(from Bolsena km. 3.8)
❱ 🖷 0761/798738
PINETA
Via A. Diaz
❱ 0761/799801

VAL DI SOLE
km. 117.8 on the Cassia
(from Bolsena Km. 4.8)
❱ 0761/797064 🖷 0761/798698
VILLAGGIO CAMPING LIDO
km. 111.5 on the Cassia
(from Bolsena km. 1.6)
❱ 0761/799258 🖷 0761/796105

Montefiascone
AMALASUNTA
deviation km. 98 on the Cassia
(from Montefiascone km. 5)
❱ 0761/825494 🖷 0761/826304

Capodimonte
BISENZIO
km. 13 str. Verentana
(from Capodimonte km. 1)
❱ 0761/872507

San Lorenzo Nuovo
MARIO
deviation km. 119.7 on the Cassia
(from San Lorenzo Nuovo km. 4.6)
❱ 0763/727485

VACATION HOMES
Bolsena
S. MARIA DEL GIGLIO
Via Madonna del Giglio, 49
❱ 🖷 0761/799066

Montefiascone
ACCOGLIENZA
"RAGGIO DI SOLE"
Via San Francesco, 3
❱ 0761/826142
CENTRO DELLA SPIRITUALITÀ
SANTA LUCIA FILIPPINI
Via Santa Maria in Arce, 11
❱ 0761/826088

Capodimonte
SACRO CUORE
Viale Regina Margherita, 42
❱ 0761/870051 🖷 0761/872552

RESTAURANTS-TRATTORIAS
PIZZERIAS
Bolsena
AI PLATANI
Via Roma, 2 ❱ 0761/798787

ANGELA E PIERO
Via della Rena, 98) 0761/799264
BELLA PIZZA
Via Marconi, 10) 0761/799904
DA GUIDO
Viale Armando Diaz, 1) 0761/799106
DA PICCHIETTO
Via Porta Fiorentina, 15
) 🖳 0761/799158
IL GABBIANO
Viale Cadorna, 2) 0761/799142
IL TOSCANO
Piazzale Gramsci, 19) 0761/799054
LA CONCHIGLIA
Viale Colesanti, 27
) 0761/799009 🖳 0761/798172
LA FORNACELLA
S.S. Cassia Km. 111) 0761/798054
LA PINETA
Viale Diaz, 48) 0761/796021
LA SIRENETTA
Viale Cadorna, 8) 🖳 0761/799096
LA TAVERNETTA
Corso Cavour, 54) 0761/798979
LA VECCHIA CANTINA
Vicolo S. Giorgio, 23) 0761/798603
LE NAIADI SUL LAGO
Viale Cadorna, 95) 0761/799017
LIDO
S.S. Cassia km. 114.8
) 0761/799026 🖳 0761/794879
VERDE LUNA snc
Via Roma) 0761/799023
TAKE AWAY PIZZERIA
Corso Repubblica, 57
) 0761/798963
TRATTORIA PIZZERIA DEL MORO
Piazzale D. Alighieri, 15
) 0761/798810

Montefiascone
BORSARI
Via Bandita, 25) 0761/826068
LA CARAVELLA
Via del Lago, 79) 0761/826843
PER BACCO
Via XXIV Maggio, 53) 0761/825777
PIZZERIA ARCOBALENO
Via Salotti Cardinale, 33
) 0761/820750
PIZZERIA DA EDOARDO
Via Dante Alighieri, 26
) 0761/826185

PIZZERIA DA IVALDO
Via del Lago, 118) 0761/825089
RISTORANTE IL CAMINETTO
Via Cassia Nord, km. 102
) 0761/826486
RISTORANTE DA ALFREDO
Via Cassia, 83) 0761/826255
RISTORANTE DA RITA
Via Santa Maria delle Grazie, 5
) 0761/826710
RISTORANTE IL CAPITANO
Via Verentana, 18) 0761/820833
RISTORANTE-PIZZERIA BORGO ANTICO
Corso Cavour, 20) 0761/834019
SFIZIO PIZZA
Via Cassia Vecchia, 9) 0761/830083
TRATTORIA DA ALVARO
Via Bandita, 53) 0761/826130
TRATTORIA DA MORANO
Via del Lago, 60) 0761/826394
TRATTORIA MIRALAGO
Via Bandita, 15) 0761/826231
TRATTORIA "DA CORRADO"
Via del Lago, 152) 0761/826996

Marta
DA GINO AL MIRALAGO
Lungolago G. Marconi, 58
) 🖳 0761/870910
PIZZERIA LA PINETA
Via Elmo Chiatti, 2) 0761/872353
RISTORANTE DA OTELLO
Via Laertina, 5
) 🖳 0761/871627
RISTORANTE IL GIRASOLE
Località Caraso
) 0761/871448
RISTORANTE IL PIRATA
Via della Spiaggia, 3
) 0761/871515
RISTORANTE S. EGIDIO
Via Giuseppe Garibaldi, 80
) 0761/871543
TRATTORIA DELLA IOLANDA
Via Amalasunta, 94
) 0761/871504

Capodimonte
DA MASSIMO
Via Gradoli, 11) 0761/870148
LA BISENTINA
Viale Regina Margherita, 56
) 0761/870331

LA PIROGA
Via San Sebastiano, 9
☏ 0761/870780
RISTORANTE DA ELIO
Via Annibalcaro, 37
☏ 0761/873000
RIVA BLU
Via Regina Margherita, 7
☏ 🖳 0761/870255

Valentano
LOCANDA LA VOLTARELLA
Via Solferino, 25
☏ 0761/422197
RISTORANTE "LA CIOTOLA"
Via della Villa, 27
☏ 0761/422132

Gradoli
LA RIPETTA
Via Roma, 38 ☏ 0761/456100
RISTORANTE LA GRATA
Località La Grata, 9
☏ 0761/456552
TRATTORIA DA GIGGETTO
Località Montesanano
☏ 0761/456138

TRATTORIA-PIZZERIA
"LA PERGOLA"
Via del Macello, 11 ☏ 0761/456345

Grotte di Castro
RISTORANTE LE SIRENE
Località Borghetto ☏ 0763/727733
TITTI PIZZA
Via Vittorio Veneto, 17 ☏ 0763/797285

San Lorenzo Nuovo
GIGANTOPIZZA
Via delle Cantine, 3 ☏ 0763/727132
IL MERLO PARLANTE
Via Acquapendente, 15
☏ 0763/727666
'L PIGNATTO
Via Luigi Turchetti, 6 ☏ 0763/726032
RISTORANTE - PIZZERIA "TAMURÈ"
Località Oppietti ☏ 🖳 0763/727476
RISTORANTE PAESE VECCHIO
Via del Mascherone, 1
☏ 0763/727106
STELLA SUL LAGO
Località Prati Renari ☏ 0763/727484
TRATTORIA DA MILLO
Località Prati Renari ☏ 0763/727300

The Publishing House wishes to thank Dr. Pietro Tamburini, director of the Museo Territoriale del Lago di Bolsena, for his priceless collaboration.

© Copyright 2004 by Bonechi - Edizioni "Il Turismo" S.r.l.
Via Giuseppe di Vittorio, 31 - 50145 Florence
Tel. +39-055.37.57.39
Fax +39-055.37.47.01
E-mail: bbonechi@dada.it
info@bonechionline.com
http://www.bonechionline.com
All rights reserved
Printed in Italy
Publishing editor: Barbara Bonechi
Graphic design and layout: Sabrina Menicacci
Cover, maps and photo retouching: Paola Rufino
Text revision and iconographic research: Lorena Lazzari
English translation: Erika Pauli for Studio Comunicare
Photographs: Archives of the Publishing House, Claudio Tini,
Giancarlo Breccola, Luigi Mecorio, Giuseppe Di Sorte.
Foto Palozzi: pagg. 40-65-66, SMA concessione n. 119 del 18/02/94
Photolithography: QIP pscrl, Florence
Printed by: Petruzzi Stampa, Città di Castello (PG)
ISBN: 88-7204-544-4

* The location of the artworks in this book corresponds to their whereabouts as the book goes to press

Index

Concessionary agent for Lazio (excluding Rome):
Archidee di Claudio Tini
Località Sant'Egidio - 01032 Caprarola (VT)
Tel. and Fax +39-0761.647540
e-mail: archi@thunder.it